TABLE OF CONTENTS

For the Teacher

This reproducible study guide to use in conjunction with the novel *Touching Spirit Bear* consists of lessons for guided reading. Written in chapter-by-chapter format, the guide contains a synopsis, pre-reading activities, vocabulary and comprehension exercises, as well as extension activities to be used as follow-up to the novel.

In a homogeneous classroom, whole class instruction with one title is appropriate. In a heterogeneous classroom, reading groups should be formed: each group works on a different novel at its reading level. Depending upon the length of time devoted to reading in the classroom, each novel, with its guide and accompanying lessons, may be completed in three to six weeks.

Begin using NOVEL-TIES for reading development by distributing the novel and a folder to each child. Distribute duplicated pages of the study guide for students to place in their folders. After examining the cover and glancing through the book, students can participate in several pre-reading activities. Vocabulary questions should be considered prior to reading a chapter unit; all other work should be done after the chapter has been read. Comprehension questions can be answered orally or in writing. The classroom teacher should determine the amount of work to be assigned, always keeping in mind that readers must be nurtured and that the ultimate goal is encouraging students' love of reading.

The benefits of using NOVEL-TIES are numerous. Students read good literature in the original, rather than in abridged or edited form. The good reading habits, formed by practice in focusing on interpretive comprehension and literary techniques, will be transferred to the books students read independently. Passive readers become active, avid readers.

SYNOPSIS

Cole Matthews has been in trouble for years, but when he breaks into a hardware store and badly beats the boy who turns him in, his own life is in danger. Cole faces a jail sentence for assaulting Peter Driscal, now in the hospital with complications from the beating. Cole's parents turn away from him, the community wants him locked up: it seems that nobody can see any good in this troubled fifteen-year-old.

Then Cole is offered an alternative to prison time. He can apply for Native American Circle Justice, a system that seeks to heal both the criminal and the victims of the crime. In Cole's case, serving a sentence under Circle Justice would mean a year's banishment to a remote Alaskan island. And he can only participate in this program if he finds a sponsor, someone with the authority to supervise him during his term. He finds a sponsor in Garvey, his probation officer. Despite Cole's anger and resistance to help, Garvey seems to think the boy is worth saving.

Along with Edwin, the elder of the Tlingit tribe, Garvey and Cole make their way to the island. Cole is on his own, provided only with a shelter and supplies. Despite all the good advice of Garvey and Edwin, the boy seems doomed to destroy himself. In a fit of rage he burns down his cabin and tosses aside the ceremonial blanket left to keep him warm. Worst of all, he tries to kill the powerful white Spirit Bear of the island. But the huge bear mauls Cole and leaves him bleeding and crippled on the ground. Cole manages to survive a long night of suffering in the wild storm that sweeps the island.

Cole is rescued and recuperates in a mainland hospital for six months. During this time, he thinks about the lessons he has learned during his brief, traumatic visit to the island. He realizes that as the child of a physically abusive father and a frightened mother, he has developed a rage that he must control if he wants to save his own life.

Emerging battered and confused from the hospital, Cole once again faces jail time. He is able to persuade the members of the Justice Circle to give him another chance to serve his year's banishment on the island. This time, his challenge will be even more difficult. He must build his own shelter with his partly disabled body and constantly prove to Garvey and Edwin that their trust in him is justified. Cole begins to accept the wisdom of these men. He learns their dances and thoughtful ways, although these sometimes bewilder him. He learns that he is responsible for his own actions and emotions, and that he can forgive himself along with those who wronged him. But can he earn the forgiveness of Peter Driscal, the boy he almost killed?

When Peter Driscal tries to commit suicide in the long depression that followed the beating, nobody knows how to help. It is Cole who offers the hope that the island will heal Peter as it has helped to heal him. When Peter comes to the island, he faces his own ordeal of anger and pain, and finally discovers that he, too, can forgive what has been done to him. So the healing circle closes, giving each boy new hope for the future.

BACKGROUND INFORMATION

The Tlingit Indians

The Tlingit, a Native-American tribe that ranges from Canada to Southeast Alaska, are fishermen, artists, and storytellers. The Tlingit have always built their villages facing the sea, which gives them halibut, salmon, clams, and other delicacies. The forests of the region yield berries and other edible vegetation. Because food gathering and hunting did not occupy all of their time, early Tlingit culture developed rapidly, outstripping that of their neighbors, the Aleuts. The Tlingit skillfully constructed wooden houses, boats, and canoes. The people traditionally devoted themselves to woodcarving and other arts, including ceremonial dances and an extensive oral literature.

The society of the Tlingit was highly organized. The clan, or extended family, was the most important social unit. Children of a clan had many "parents," people who looked after their welfare and taught them the Tlingit ways. In winter, clan members shared large houses. The women did the cooking for their families at a large fire pit, alongside the other women of the clan. During these months, the people hunted and trapped food and worked at native crafts such as baskets and blanket weaving, tool carving, and canoe building. In summer, the Tlingit set up fish camps, moving from stream to stream in pursuit of different kinds of salmon. Individual streams were owned by the different clans, with others having to ask permission to fish in those waters.

The Tlingit have always seen their relation to nature as a partnership. They worship animal gods and carve their images on ceremonial totem poles. The early Tlingit carved an animal on his fishing hook, believing that the fish would be easier to catch under the influence of some mighty animal's spirit. Today, the people still respect the place of each living thing in the natural cycle.

Many of the stories from Tlingit culture have to do with animals. Raven, one of the best-loved creatures of the Tlingit, is believed to have played a major role in the creation of the earth's resources. Raven is also a trickster, and many amusing tales of his predicaments can be found in Tlingit literature. Eagle, Frog, and Wolf are also important figures in Tlingit storytelling.

In *Touching Spirit Bear*, the Tlingit elder Edwin encourages Cole to carve different animals into his totem pole. In early Tlingit culture, individual clans had ownership of the particular animal designs depicted in paintings and woodcarvings. These were called "crest animals." The crest animals of a clan might be a frog, a bird, a bear, or any other creature of the area. Today, because many outsiders are interested in buying Tlingit paintings and carvings, production has become much more commercial. For the first time, artists are making these objects with the idea of selling them outside the community, rather than for ceremonial purposes. Inevitably, contact with the world beyond their villages has brought some changes to the Tlingit people, but many still hold fast to their traditional customs and beliefs.

PRE-READING ACTIVITIES AND DISCUSSION QUESTIONS

1. Preview the book by reading the title and the author's name and by looking at the illustration on the cover. What do you think the story will be about? Where and when do you think it takes place?

2. **Social Studies Connection:** Read the Background Information on page two of this study guide and do some additional research to learn more about the Tlingit Indians. Brainstorm with a group of classmates to fill in a K-W-L chart, such as the one below. Jot down what you already know in the first column. List your questions in the second column. When you finish the book, record what you learned in the third column.

What I Know –K–	What I Want to Learn –W–	What I Learned –L–

3. **Social Studies Connection:** On a map or globe locate the places on Cole's route from Minneapolis to Seattle; on to Ketchikan, Alaska; and finally on to the Tlingit village of Drake. About how many miles did Cole have to travel between Minneapolis and his destination? As you read the novel consider how great is the distance, both physically and emotionally, between the beginning and the end of his journey.

4. **Cooperative Learning Activity:** With your classmates, discuss books and films in which the main character must survive an ordeal of the body and spirit. Make a list of these books and films, including any details about setting or conflict that you recall. Compare your list with those of your classmates.

5. Cole Matthews, the main character in this novel, has several important conflicts he must resolve. What kinds of conflicts have you experienced in your own life? With a group of classmates, discuss these conflicts and brainstorm ways in which such problems might be settled.

6. Find some pictures of the Alaskan wilderness and the animals that inhabit the region. Display these pictures on the classroom bulletin board as you and your classmates read the book.

7. Do some research to find out how our legal system handles criminal cases involving juvenile offenders. Then answer the following questions:
    *   What happens in the court system when a young person commits a crime?
    *   What options does our legal system provide when helping to rehabilitate a youthful offender?
    *   Which alternatives seem most likely to help a troubled teen live a better life?

8. The main character in the story has to set some major goals for himself in order to change the direction of his life. What kinds of goals have you set for yourself? Make a list of three goals that you hope to reach.

9. Read aloud the opening paragraph with other students reading the same book. What information have you learned about the main character and the setting of this book?

CHAPTERS 1 – 5

Vocabulary: Synonyms are words with similar meanings. Draw a line from each word in column A to its synonym in column B. Then use the words in column A to fill in the blanks in the sentence below.

	A		B
1.	reluctantly	a.	distant
2.	feigned	b.	final
3.	banishment	c.	abate
4.	subside	d.	hesitantly
5.	remote	e.	pretended
6.	ultimate	f.	meekness
7.	humility	g.	foreboding
8.	omen	h.	exile

. . . .

1. As the prisoner awaited sentencing he wondered whether imprisonment would be worse than _____ to a small island.

2. The black clouds are a(n) _____ of an approaching storm.

3. The _____ goal of everyone on the track team is to win a gold medal.

4. The children had so much fun at the party that they left _____.

5. Because of his _____, not even old friends knew of his heroic rescues aboard a sinking ship.

6. As the floodwaters began to _____, people returned to their damaged homes.

7. In the well-known folk tale, the wolf _____ friendliness to fool Little Red Riding Hood.

8. It is amazing how each year the same colorful birds return to our _____ island, far from the mainland.

> Read to find out why Cole Matthews was left alone to survive on an island.

Chapters 1 – 5 (cont.)

Questions:

1. Why was Cole Matthews facing an entire year alone in southeast Alaska?

2. Why wasn't Cole worried about the terms of his punishment?

3. Why had Cole attacked Peter Driscal?

4. In what basic way was Native American Circle Justice different from the standard system of justice?

5. What did Edwin mean when he warned Cole that he was part of a "much bigger circle" on the island?

6. Why did Garvey hesitate before becoming Cole's sponsor?

7. Why did Cole burn down his shelter?

8. Why had Garvey asked Cole to taste each ingredient before sampling the cake?

9. Why were the decisions made at the healing circle important to Cole?

10. Why did Cole return to the island after attempting escape?

Questions for Discussion:

1. Why do you think Circle Justice was offered to Cole as an alternative to a prison term? Do you think it might be a successful alternative for Cole?

2. Do you think Cole's parents were the cause of their son's violence, or did Cole share responsibility for his behavior?

3. Why might the island be a good place for a person like Cole to find himself? Can you think of any other place that might serve the same purpose?

4. Why do you think Garvey agreed to be Cole's sponsor?

Literary Elements:

I. *Setting*—Setting refers to the time and place where the events of a novel occur. What is the setting of *Touching Spirit Bear*?

_____

What impactd does the setting have on the events that happen in the novel?

_____

_____

Chapters 1 – 5 (cont.)

II. *Conflict*—In a work of literature, a conflict is a struggle between opposing forces. It may be the struggle of a person against society, a person battling against nature, or a person's inner struggle. Use a chart, such as the one below, to record the conflicts that appear in *Touching Spirit Bear*. Add to the chart as you continue to read the book.

Type of Conflict	Example
person *vs.* person/society	
person *vs.* nature	
person *vs.* self (inner struggle)	

Literary Devices:

I. *Flashback*—A flashback in a narrative refers to a scene that does not follow the time order of the plot. The flashback describes an event or events that took place in the past. What did the flashback that related the events at the first healing circle add to Cole's story?

II. *Personification*—Personification is a figure of speech in which an author grants human characteristics to nonhuman objects. For example:

> With every stroke forward, a giant invisible hand had pushed him
> two strokes backward into the bay, returning him toward the shore.

What is being personified?

Why is this more vivid than saying "The current was too strong for him and he could not fight it"?

Chapters 1 – 5 (cont.)

III. *Symbol*—A symbol in literature is a person, object, or event that represents an idea or a set of ideas. What does the Spirit Bear symbolize?

_____

_____

What might the at.óow symbolize?

_____

_____

Social Studies Connection:

Research some other Native-American traditions. Choose a tradition or custom that interests you and compare it to a practice in your own culture. Prepare an oral report that shows how the two traditions are similar and different.

Writing Activity:

Write about a time when a strong emotion ruled your actions. What happened as a result of this powerful feeling?

CHAPTERS 6 – 9

Vocabulary: Draw a line from each word on the left to its definition on the right. Then use the numbered words to fill in the blanks in the sentences below.

1. rigid   a. attack
2. symptoms   b. stormy
3. assault   c. beat-up; bruised
4. incessant   d. signs or indications of something
5. mauled   e. turned aside from
6. turbulent   f. persuaded
7. deflected   g. stiff
8. coaxed   h. without stopping

. . . .

1. The _____ waters of the ocean made swimming and boating impossible.

2. The skilled hockey player at the goal neatly _____ the puck with a single motion of his hockey stick.

3. With promises to clean my room and walk the dog, I finally _____ my parents into letting me go to the concert.

4. The _____ rain kept us indoors for an entire day.

5. Fever and aching muscles are common _____ of the flu.

6. The townspeople piled up sand bags to protect themselves against the _____ of the flooding river.

7. My body became _____ with fear, making it impossible for me to dive off the high board.

8. A fierce lion _____ its prey and dragged it home to feed its young.

Read to find out how Cole faced problems of survival once he arrived on the island.

Chapters 6 – 9 (cont.)

Questions:

1. Why did Garvey argue that they needed to find solutions to problems such as the ones Cole experienced?

2. Why did Cole's mother quickly pass the feather to Garvey when Cole insisted she admit the truth about his father's violence?

3. Why did Cole spend time studying the tides?

4. Why didn't Cole appreciate the beauty of the northern lights?

5. Why had Cole expected the giant bear to run away from him?

6. What helped Cole to survive the long night after the bear's attack?

7. What event revealed Cole's developing concern and compassion for other living things in his world?

Questions for Discussion:

1. In what ways might Cole be a symptom of problems within the community where he lives?

2. What do you think a person could learn from a vision quest? Why did Garvey think this might be part of the solution for Cole?

3. Why do you think Cole was determined to kill the Spirit Bear?

4. Do you know someone who never takes responsibility for his or her actions? How does such an attitude affect this person's relationship with others?

Literary Devices:

I. *Metaphor*—A metaphor is a suggested or implied comparison between two unlike objects. For example:

> . . . on his [Cole's] right stood a dressed-up puppet, afraid of her own shadow.

What is being compared?

_____

Why is this an apt comparison?

_____

_____

Chapters 6 – 9 (cont.)

II. *Simile*—A simile is a figure of speech that compares two unlike objects using the words "like" or "as" For example:

Tonight, raw feelings have been exposed like plowed-up ground. . .

What is being compared?

_____

Why is this better then saying, "People displayed their strong feelings"?

_____

III. *Flashback*—Why do you think the novel often flashes back to episodes that occurred prior to Cole's island experience?

_____

_____

IV. *Personification*—What is being personified in the following example?

Curtains of northern lights danced wildly under the Big Dipper.

_____

How does this make the scene vivid and reflect Cole's state of mind?

_____

_____

Writing Activity:

Write about a time when you were able to care more about another person or animal even more than yourself. Describe the situation and explain how caring about another made you feel.

CHAPTERS 10 – 15

Vocabulary: Antonyms are words with opposite meanings. Draw a line from each word in column A to its antonym in column B. Then use the words in Column A to complete the sentences below.

	A		B
1.	detached	a.	ordinary
2.	relinquish	b.	varied
3.	bizarre	c.	cheerful
4.	monotonous	d.	saved
5.	dismal	e.	keep
6.	insignificant	f.	connected
7.	inevitable	g.	important
8.	squandered	h.	unexpected

. . . .

1. The speaker's voice was so _____ that many in the audience fell asleep.

2. After my little sister saw the basket of adorable kittens, it was _____ that she should want one for a pet.

3. The nurse flung open the window and let light and a sweet breeze into the patient's _____ room.

4. After the child _____ his allowance on candy, he realized he should have saved some money for more important things.

5. The judge warned the jury to focus on important information and ignore _____ details.

6. You will look _____ if you wear a ski jacket to the beach on a hot summer day.

7. Don't _____ your hold on that leash, or the dog will dash through the park and chase all the squirrels.

8. Having been away for years, I felt _____ from my family's celebrations and their difficulties.

> Read to find out whether Cole survived the bear attack.

Chapters 10 – 15 (cont.)

Questions:

1. Why did Cole identify with the baby sparrows?

2. What did Cole suddenly realize about power, now that he had so little?

3. Why did Cole spit at the Spirit Bear when it returned?

4. What made Cole come to face death with contentment?

5. What did the dream about the monsters reveal about Cole's state of mind?

6. How did Cole get off the island?

7. Why did Edwin tell Cole, "A person is never done being mad"?

8. Why did Cole's mother agree to press charges against Cole's father for child abuse? How did her actions help the healing process for the family?

9. Why was Cole allowed to finish his term under the Circle Justice program?

10. What happened to convince Edwin and Garvey that Cole's story about the Spirit Bear was true?

Questions for Discussion:

1. What elements of his personality do you think allowed Cole to survive his two-day ordeal on the island?

2. Why do you suppose it was important for Cole to touch the Spirit Bear?

3. Do you think Garvey was guilty for any of Cole's pain and suffering? What was significant about Cole's admission to Garvey that the bear attack was his own fault?

4. Why do you think the narrative jumped ahead by six months after Cole's rescue?

5. Do you think Cole could have experienced a profound personality change without the suffering that occurred because of the bear attack? Do you think Cole's mother could have changed if her son had not come so near death?

6. Why do you suppose that Edwin and Garvey still believed Cole was worth saving, even after he burned down the shelter and tried to kill the bear?

Literary Devices:

I. *Symbolism*—How does the charred tree function as a symbol? What does that tree represent to Cole?

_____

_____

Chapters 10 – 15 (cont.)

II. *Irony*—Irony in literature refers to a twist of fate or a situation that is the opposite of that which is expected. What is ironic about the moment when Cole became determined to live?

_____

_____

Literary Element: Characterization

What traits of character allowed Cole to survive the experience of the bear attack? How were these same traits a destructive force in Cole's life prior to the bear attack?

_____

_____

_____

Science Connection:

Do some research about wildlife in Alaska. Write a report about some of the interesting or unusual species of plants and animals found there.

Writing Activities:

1. Notice the sensory detail as you reread the description of Cole as he experienced the aftermath of the bear attack. Write a description of your emotional and physical condition after a significant event in your life.

2. Write a chapter that explains what happens to Cole in the six months between his arrival at the hospital and the day when he finally is able to walk out of the hospital.

CHAPTERS 16 – 20

Vocabulary: Analogies are equations in which the first pair of words has the same relationship as the second pair of words. For example: RUSH is to HURRY as QUARREL is to ARGUE. Both pairs of words are synonyms. Choose the best word from the Word Box to complete each of the analogies below.

```
                          WORD BOX
         deliberately      skiff          warily
         fester            suspend        weary
         potential         vulnerable
```

1. _____ is to BOAT as DIESEL is to TRAIN.

2. CUT is to BLEED as SORE is to _____.

3. WEAK is to _____ as STRONG is to IMPERVIOUS.

4. ENERGETIC is to _____ as SHARP is to DULL.

5. FULFILL is to DREAM as ACHIEVE is to _____.

6. HANG is to _____ CLIMB is to ASCEND.

7. TRUSTINGLY is to _____ as FEARFULLY is to BRAVELY.

8. _____ is to CRIME as THOUGHTLESSLY is to ACCIDENT.

> Read to find out whether Garvey will leave Cole alone on the island.

Questions:

1. Why was Cole's second attempt to live on the island more challenging than the first?

2. What did Garvey mean when he told Cole, "You're going to prove your commitment"?

3. What was Garvey trying to teach Cole through the example of the hot dog?

4. Why didn't Edwin and Garvey help Cole with the difficult task of building the shelter?

5. According to Edwin, why was the Tlingit healing process better than psychological counseling?

Chapters 16 – 20 (cont.)

6. What was Cole supposed to learn from carrying the rock up the hill?

7. Why did Garvey and Edwin allow Cole to remain on the island?

8. What gave Edwin and Garvey a deep understanding of Cole's problems?

9. What did Cole experience in the cold pond when he bathed in it alone?

Questions for Discussion:

1. Why do you suppose that the simple exercises Cole learned from the two older men helped him more than the psychological counseling he had received in Minnesota?

2. Why do you think dancing, as Edwin and Garvey modeled, could have a healing function?

3. Do you think Garvey and Edwin should have been less demanding and more helpful to Cole?

4. What do you think is the one thing that Garvey wanted Cole to discover for himself once he was alone on the island?

Cooperative Learning Activity:

Work with a small group of your classmates to discuss the questions that follow. Record your group's responses. Compare your responses with those of other groups in your classroom.

- What are some of the ways that people learn about themselves and the world around them? Which of these ways seem to make the strongest impression?

- Why couldn't Cole seem to learn from most of the people he had known—his parents, peers, and teachers?

- Will Cole be able to master his anger and reclaim his life?

Music/Dance Connection

Create a dance based upon the spirit and actions of an animal you admire. Set your dance to music and perform it for a group of classmates. Be sure to do this in an atmosphere of acceptance and respect for others' creativity.

Writing Activity:

Imagine that you are Cole and write a letter to your mother explaining how you are dealing with your anger and fears. Explain how the lessons of the island and your two sponsors are helping you to heal physically and emotionally.

CHAPTERS 21 – 24

Vocabulary: Use the context to figure out the meaning of the underlined word in each of the following sentences. Then compare your answer with one you find in a dictionary.

1. We <u>savored</u> the hot, hearty soup, eating slowly and then asking for a second bowl.

   Your definition_____

   Dictionary definition _____

2. The atmosphere of the large store was <u>hectic</u>, as shoppers rushed around looking for holiday gifts and bargains.

   Your definition_____

   Dictionary definition _____

3. Our teacher asked each student to make a family tree that showed his or her <u>ancestry</u>.

   Your definition_____

   Dictionary definition _____

4. I was in no particular hurry, so I <u>meandered</u> by the river, enjoying the beauty of the day.

   Your definition_____

   Dictionary definition _____

5. When offered a plate of vegetables, the child <u>grimaced</u> and asked for a piece of pie instead.

   Your definition_____

   Dictionary definition _____

6. With his usual <u>ingenuity</u>, my brother built a spaceship out of cardboard boxes and aluminum cans.

   Your definition_____

   Dictionary definition _____

> Read to find out whether Cole completes his healing process.

Chapters 21 – 24 (cont.)

Questions:

1. How did Cole's behavior show that he took pride in his shelter on the island?

2. Why did Cole have frightening thoughts when he looked at the huge log?

3. How did performing the eagle dance help Cole master his mind and body?

4. Why wasn't Edwin furious when he saw that Cole had first tried to shape the log into a canoe?

5. According to Edwin, how are creating a totem pole and a dance similar?

6. Why did Cole try to erase his own scent and make himself invisible?

7. At what moment did Cole know he was ready to do the anger dance?

8. What was the lesson Cole had to learn on his own before he could successfully heal?

Questions for Discussion:

1. Why do you suppose Cole was able to resist the temptation to build the canoe? What did his choice reveal about his state of mind?

2. Why do you think the dance of anger was the final dance Cole had to create?

3. Who do you think Cole was forgiving as he completed his anger dance?

4. Why do you think Edwin seemed disappointed in Cole?

Literary Devices: Cliffhanger

A cliffhanger is an episode that ends at a suspenseful point in a story. Cliffhangers usually are placed at the end of a chapter. What is the cliffhanger at the end of Chapter Twenty-Four?

Art Connection:

Do some research to find out about Native American totem poles. Then design your own totem pole, using wood, paint, clay, or other materials. Give a talk about how you made your totem pole and tell what the images represent.

Writing Activities:

1. Imagine that you are Cole's mother. Write a letter to Cole expressing your feelings for him and filling him in on what is happening in the community during his absence.

2. What animal best represents your spirit? Write a description of this animal that captures its appearance, behavior, habits, and overall spirit. Explain why you feel a kinship with this particular animal.

CHAPTERS 25 – 28

Vocabulary: Use the words in the word box and the clues below to complete the crossword puzzle.

WORD BOX			
clenched	frigid	massive	rehabilitation
crouched	glisten	mesmerize	sarcasm
distinct	hoarse	pleaded	taunt
			wavered

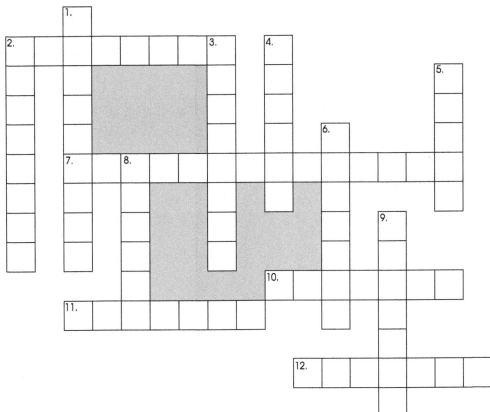

Across
2. gripped tightly
7. restoration to a condition of good health
10. showed indecision
11. begged
12. gleam

Down
1. hypnotize
2. stooped; bent low
3. not identical
4. very cold in temperature
5. tease; provoke
6. bulky and heavy
8. having a husky or rough vocal tone
9. harsh or bitter ridicule

Read to find out if Cole is able to help Peter heal.

Chapters 25 – 28 (cont.)

Questions:

1. Why did Cole suggest that Peter come to the island?

2. Why did Peter's family and the members of the Circle take the risk of leaving Peter on the island with Cole?

3. Why did Edwin want Cole to tell Peter and his parents about everything that had happened to him since he arrived on the island?

4. Why did Peter at first refuse Cole's help?

5. Why didn't Cole try to defend himself against Peter's attack?

6. Why did Cole give the at.óow, his most valued possession, to Peter?

Questions for Discussion:

1. Why do you think Peter had to physically assault Cole before he could begin to forgive him?

2. Why might the Spirit Bear have come to the pond on the day Peter attacked Cole? What did the appearance of the bear mean to the two boys?

3. How do you think Cole and Peter might relate to each other in the future? How might their story continue?

Literary Element: Hero and Anti-Hero

A *hero* is a person who can be admired. A hero, or heroine, can be the main character of a story. An *anti-hero* is a person or literary character who does not conform to society's ideas of what is correct and moral. Now that you have read the novel, try to decide whether Cole Matthews is a hero or an anti-hero. Which other characters in the novel show aspects of heroism?

Writing Activities:

1. Write about a time when you forgave somebody who hurt or angered you. What happened during this experience? How was the situation resolved?

2. Write a brief plot outline describing an adventure the two boys might share in the future.

CLOZE ACTIVITY:

The following excerpt is taken from Chapter Five. Read it through completely and then go back and fill in the blank spaces with words that make sense. When you have finished you may compare your language with that of the author.

Once clear of the bay, Cole swam even harder. Misty rain roughed the water as waves _____1_____ over his head. When he stopped to _____2_____, his breath came in ragged gasps. His _____3_____ limbs felt wooden and stiff, moving awkwardly _____4_____ if disconnected from his body. Cole turned _____5_____ look back.

At first his mind rejected _____6_____ he saw—he was still at the _____7_____ of the bay. He shook his head _____8_____ clear the illusion, but it was no _____9_____. This was the same spot he had _____10_____ at a thousand strokes earlier. But how _____11_____ it be? The wind and waves hadn't _____12_____ that strong, yet even as he struggled _____13_____ tread water with his numb limbs, he _____14_____ himself drifting back toward the shoreline.

In _____15_____ instant, Cole realized his mistake. His anger _____16_____ so clouded his thinking, he hadn't considered _____17_____ incoming tide. With every stroke forward, a _____18_____ invisible hand had pushed him two strokes _____19_____ into the bay, returning him toward the _____20_____.

A sharp cramp gripped Cole's leg, then _____21_____ other leg started cramping. He gasped for _____22_____ and panicked. He had to make it _____23_____ to land. Any land. Frantically he flailed at the water.

POST-READING ACTIVITIES AND DISCUSSION QUESTIONS

1. Return to the K-W-L chart that you began in the Pre-Reading Activities on page three of this study guide. Based on your reading of the book, make any necessary corrections in the first column and write any new information that you have learned about Tlingit culture in the third column. Compare your chart with those of your classmates.

2. Imagine that you are a reporter covering Cole's case for a local Minnesota newspaper. You have interviewed Cole, Edwin, Garvey, Peter's family, and some members of the Circle, and now have all the relevant facts of the case. Write an article that deals with Cole's crime, ordeal, and rehabilitation.

3. Cole Matthews had to deal with the psychological burdens of an abusive father and an alcoholic mother. By the end of the novel, he has learned that he can make choices about his actions rather than repeat the cycle of violence. With a small group of classmates, discuss how his time on the island helped free Cole from the past.

4. Select an episode or incident from the novel and write a film script based upon that scene. As you compose your script, think about such film elements as scenery, camera angles, dialogue, narration, and acting. In your script, give directions about each of these elements.

5. **Art Connection:** Working with two other classmates, create a triptych, a three-part painting, that depicts three different events in the novel. When each section of the painting is complete, glue it to a piece of cardboard or wood. Attach the three parts with tape, staples, or brads so that the triptych tells the story of Cole Matthews.

6. **Cooperative Learning Activity:** Work with a group of classmates to plan a wilderness survival weekend. Where might you go? What supplies would be needed for this experience? What skills would be most essential? Make a written record of your discussion.

7. At the beginning of the novel, Cole Matthews is a difficult character to like. How does the author manage to make us care about what happens to him? Which events in the novel serve to make him a more sympathetic character?

8. **Literary Element: Theme** The theme in a literary work is its controlling idea. In *Touching Spirit Bear*, the author explores several important themes, such as coming to terms with the past, accepting limitations, controlling one's emotions, and accepting responsibility for one's actions. Choose one of these themes and discuss how it is worked out in the novel.

Post-Reading Activities and Discussion Questions (cont.)

9. **Literature Circle:** Have a literature circle discussion in which you tell your personal reactions to *Touching Spirit Bear*. Here are some questions and sentence starters to help your literature circle begin a discussion.

   - How are you like Cole? How are you different?
   - Do you find the characters in the novel realistic? Why or why not?
   - Which character did you like the most? The least?
   - Who else would like to read this novel? Why?
   - What questions would you like to ask the author about this novel?
   - It was not fair when . . .
   - I would have liked to see . . .
   - I wonder . . .
   - Cole learned that . . .

SUGGESTIONS FOR FURTHER READING

* Bloor, Edward. *Tangerine*. HMH Books.

* Craven, Margaret. *I Heard the Owl Call My Name*. Dell.

  Eckert, Allen. *Incident at Hawk's Hill*. Little Brown.

* George, Jean Craighead. *Julie of the Wolves*. HarperCollins.

* _____. *My Side of the Mountain*. Puffin.

* Holman, Felice. *Slake's Limbo*. Aladdin.

  Krumgold, Joseph. *...And Now Miguel*. HarperCollins.

* London, Jack. *Call of the Wild*. Dover.

  Mathieson, David. *Trial by Wilderness*. Houghton Mifflin.

  Mazer , Harry. *Snow Bound*. Laurel Leaf.

  Morey, Walter. *Angry Waters*. Gentle Ben Enterprises.

  _____. *Canyon Winter*. Gentle Ben Enterprises.

* O'Dell, Scott. *Island of the Blue Dolphins*. Houghton Mifflin Harcourt.

* Paulsen, Gary. *Dogsong*. Simon & Schuster.

* _____. *Hatchet*. Simon & Schuster.

* Speare, Elizabeth George. *Sign of the Beaver*. HMH Books.

* Sperry, Armstrong. *Call It Courage*. Aladdin.

* Taylor, Theodore. *The Cay*. Laurel Leaf.

Some Other Books by Ben Mikaelsen

Countdown. Hyperion.

Ghost of Spirit Bear. HarperCollins.

Jungle of Bones. Scholastic.

Petey. Hyperion.

Red Midnight. HarperCollins.

Sparrow Hawk Red. Hyperion.

Stranded. Hyperion.

Tree Girl. HarperCollins.

* NOVEL-TIES Study Guides are available for these titles.

ANSWER KEY

Chapters 1 – 5

Vocabulary: 1. d 2. e 3. h 4. c 5. a 6. b 7. f 8. g; 1. banishment 2. omen 3. ultimate 4. reluctantly 5. humility 6. subside 7. feigned 8. remote

Questions: 1. Cole Matthews had accepted Circle Justice which meant facing an entire year alone on an island in Alaska: this form of judicial punishment was an alternative to a prison term. 2. Cole wasn't worried about spending a year on the island because he thought he could escape before he had to serve his entire term. As he looked at his past, he had always managed to avoid detention and fool those who tried to help him. 3. Cole had attacked Peter Driscal because Peter had identified Cole to the police as the person who robbed and trashed a hardware store. 4. Circle Justice concentrated on healing the criminal rather than on punishment. The healing process would relate to the crime and aim at developing moral strength and integrity. 5. When Edwin warned Cole he was part of a "much bigger circle" on the island, he meant that Cole would have to learn to live with all the other living things on the island. If he lived in harmony with plant and animal life, he would survive. 6. Garvey hesitated before becoming Cole's sponsor because he doubted the youth's sincerity about wanting to change. 7. Cole burned down his shelter because he was angry and did not know how to control himself. 8. Garvey had Cole taste each separate ingredient before tasting the cake so that he could see that life was made up of bitter and sweet elements, like the cake; the finished cake showed that there was a place for each ingredient, or element, in a person's life and that the finished product could be good in the end. 9. The people who attended the healing Circle would determine whether Cole was a candidate for Circle Justice. 10. After trying in vain to escape from the island by swimming against the current that was moving toward shore, Cole, now an injured and exhausted young man, rode the tide back to the island.

Chapters 6 – 9

Vocabulary: 1. g 2. d 3. a 4. h 5. c 6. b 7. e 8. f; 1. turbulent 2. deflected 3. coaxed 4: incessant 5. symptoms 6. assault 7. rigid 8. mauled

Questions: 1. Garvey argued that Cole's problems were not only his own but were a reflection of an ailing family and community. If they were to fail to solve problems such as those suffered by Cole, the entire society would be a victim. 2. Cole's mother quickly passed the feather to Garvey when Cole insisted that she tell the truth about his father's violence because she did not dare to lie with the feather of truth in her hand, and she feared her violent former husband. 3. Cole studied the tides so that on his next attempt to leave the island he would begin his swim on an outgoing tide. 4. Cole didn't appreciate the beauty of the northern lights because his anger and self-involvement prevented him from seeing beauty in any form. 5. Cole had expected the giant bear to run away from him because he was used to scaring or intimidating everyone around him with his threats and shows of violence 6. Cole survived the long night after the bear's attack by remembering the warmth of the ceremonial blanket, and the vision of the moon, which conjured up the healing qualities of the circles of Native American justice. 7. When Cole asked the baby birds if they were okay, he revealed that he was developing concern and compassion for other living beings.

Chapters 10 – 15

Vocabulary: 1. f 2. e 3. a 4. b 5. c 6. g 7. h 8. d; 1. monotonous 2. inevitable 3. dismal 4. squandered 5. insignificant 6. bizarre 7. relinquish 8. detached

Questions: 1. In his mental and physical state after the bear attack, Cole identified with the baby sparrows because they too were helpless and insignificant. 2. Cole suddenly realized that true power involved positive choice and finding meaning in life, while fake power was just a person's way of pretending to be in control by intimidating others. 3. In one final act of defiance Cole spat at the Spirit Bear when it returned in order to provoke it to kill him and so end his physical and emotional suffering. 4. Once Cole was able to glimpse some beauty and order in life he was able to face death with contentment. 5. Cole's dream about the monsters revealed that he still didn't fully trust himself or others. 6. Cole was rescued and taken off the island by Garvey and Edwin when they came to check on him only two days after his abandonment on the island. 7. Edwin told Cole "A person is never done being mad" because anger, like all other emotions, is part of being human and can never be eliminated, only tamed. 8. Cole's mother agreed to press child abuse charges because Garvey made her see that her silence had made her partly responsible for what had happened to her child; she could help end the cycle of violence by making Cole's father face what he had done. 9. Cole was allowed to continue his participation in Circle Justice because Garvey and Edwin decided he was worth saving and agreed to be responsible for him. 10. Edwin and Garvey began to believe Cole's story of the Spirit Bear when a man whom Edwin trusted was one of a crew who spotted a white bear on the island.

Chapters 16 – 20

Vocabulary: 1. skiff 2. fester 3. vulnerable 4. weary 5. potential 6. suspend 7. warily 8. deliberately

Questions: 1. Cole's second attempt to live on the island was more challenging than the first because he was returning with a damaged body and fears emanating from his encounter with the bear. Also, he would have to build his own shelter. 2. When Garvey told Cole, "You're going to prove your commitment" he meant that Cole would have to show them that he was both able and determined to survive on the island by his own wits and strength; he would have to cook and build an adequate shelter and learn to protect himself. 3. Through the example of the hot dog, Garvey was trying to teach Cole that a shared, joyous life is the best life; that each small moment is to be celebrated; and that each minor task is to be done as well as possible. 4. Garvey and Edwin didn't help Cole with the difficult task of building the shelter because they knew that Cole, having burned down the original cabin, would only appreciate what his own hard work could create. 5. According to Edwin, psychological counseling focused on "the left end of the stick," or the negative parts of life, whereas Tlingit healing focused on happiness and the positive contributions one could make in a lifetime. 6. From carrying the rock up the hill, Cole was supposed to learn respect for his ancestors and achieve a new awareness of how they had struggled with the burdens of daily life. 7. Garvey and Edwin decided to allow Cole to remain on the island once his actions—doing the wolf dance, bathing in the cold pond, and carrying the ancestor rock up the hill—proved his change of attitude. 8. Edwin and Garvey had a deep understanding of Cole's problems because as younger men each had struggled with anger and acted rashly and dangerously, as had Cole. 9. When he bathed alone in the cold pond, Cole experienced the ability to control his reactions and find calm; this helped him to gain a measure of self-control over his mind and his body.

Chapter 21 – 24

Vocabulary: 1. savored–enjoyed to the fullest 2. hectic–relating to a state of confused activity 3. ancestry–relation to those who came before us; forebears 4. meandered–strolled without particular purpose or destination 5. grimaced–made an expression of disgust or disapproval 6. ingenuity–cleverness; inventiveness

Questions: 1. By continuing to improve his cabin and building furniture for it, Cole showed that he took pride in his shelter. 2. When Cole looked at the huge log, he had frightening thoughts because he was tempted to build a canoe from it and not a totem pole; he had to push this thought out of his mind because he knew it would be wrong to try to escape from the island. 3. Performing the eagle dance helped Cole to master his mind by making him feel powerful and independent; it helped his body because the exertion kept his limbs from feeling stiff after his extensive injuries. 4. Edwin wasn't furious when he first saw that Cole had tried to shape the log into a canoe because Cole had, after all, conquered the urge to escape and because he admitted the brief temptation to Edwin. 5. Carving the totem and creating a dance were similar because each art form allowed Cole to explore his deepest feelings and to express himself. According to Edwin each art form allowed a person to create his own story. 6. Since wild animals are sometimes frightened off by the smell and appearance of people, Cole tried to erase his own scent and make himself invisible, hoping the Spirit Bear would show himself again. 7. At the moment when Cole felt as though he were part of the landscape; when he made himself invisible by clearing his mind; when the Spirit Bear came up to him; and after he finished a celebratory meal, Cole knew he was ready to do the anger dance. 8. Before he could heal, Cole had to discover for himself a way that he could help Peter, his former victim.

Chapters 25 – 28

Vocabulary: Across—2. clenched 7. rehabilitation 10. wavered 11. pleaded 12. glisten; Down—1. mesmerize 2. crouched 3. distinct 4. frigid 5. taunt 6. massive 8. hoarse 9. sarcasm

Questions: 1. Cole suggested that Peter come to the island because he knew how much the experience had helped him and thought it could help Peter heal, too. 2. Peter's family and the members of the Circle took the risk of leaving Peter on the island with Cole because they knew the situation was desperate; Peter had tried to kill himself and they did not know what other measures to take to protect him. 3. Edwin wanted Cole to tell Peter and his parents about everything that had happened to him since he arrived on the island because then perhaps they could see how the experience had changed Cole for the good. They could also get an idea of how the island could help Peter. 4. Peter at first refused Cole's help because he deeply distrusted and feared him. 5. Cole didn't try to defend himself against Peter's attack because he had to prove both to Peter and himself that he would no longer let his anger control him and that he would do no further harm to Peter. 6. Cole gave the at.óow to Peter as a symbol of his friendship and trust.